ONESWEETSPOT
We're not publishers.
This book is Powered by Penguins <(').

7700 Newcastle St.
New Orleans, La 70126
www.onesweetspot.com

ISBN-13: 978-0-692-38124-3
ISBN-10: 0-692-38124-4

Printed in the United States of America
10 9 8 7 6 5 4 3 2 1

First Printing: February 2015

Cover Design: Tazzico– "Cool Story Bro"
          www.tazzico.com
          @tazzico

This book is a work of the mind.
It's all true small glimpses of overly complicated experiences.
Many Apologies.

on searching for a flightless bird

For Bh.
I wish I were mature enough to tell you how I felt back in the day. We fucked up. I love you.

Prelude

Just so we're all clear…I have no idea what this is about. Well, I kind of do. Particularly, this is a collection of my own experiences.

It would be nice to say something cool like, "these experiences can be applied universally." That, of course, would be a lie.

Experiences are a personal phenomenon so private that the mere attempt at explanation is impossible. Private entities, whether they be material or intellectual, can never be public just as "black" can never be "white" and "grass" can never truly be "green."

So, truthfully, I am forced to return to my initial thesis. I have no idea what this is. It might be brilliant. It might be crap. It might be perfect. Chances are it's definitely very flawed.

I went through some stuff. I wrote this crap. Read it. Steal it. Use it.

Dickey C
www.onesweetpot.com

dickey c

The truth is…I'm honest. I guarantee you won't believe me.

dickey c

on friendship…internally

In the wake of the night come those eagerly awaiting
over-complexity in the name of simplicity. To believe in
the self is as innate as self-doubt, for self-doubt is simply
the lack of belief. For all those who believe, we rely on
you for model. For all those who doubt, we rely for the
same, but in a very opposing manner.

The strong are considered strong based on their
repetition or mimicking of others that have been deemed
strong. We gain strength by doing as the strong have
done. As we do with those who have belief. In
opposition, however, those who lack self-belief
are viewed in a highly opposing manner.

Question comes not the definition of ones character, for
that is simply based on the views of others, but in the
defining of the worth of ones self. Those who
have attained belief have done so based on a well
defined worth of the self of a model.

As the morning approaches I am begged to question my
own self-worth, my own value.
My own belief.

Repeat

As unfortunate as it may appear where sunlight is the most visible, the muses are to remain with the likes of themselves. Simply put, the best muses are the best muses.

For those destined to know have not been predetermined but, in the eyes of few, already revealed.

For those destined to rule have not been predetermined but, in the eyes of few, already revealed.

For those destined to be among the powerful have not been predetermined but, in the eyes of few, already revealed.

Knowledge is power and power ain't for everybody.

dickey c

They don't matter. They don't change…,

The possibility of wrongful thought comes just as that of wrongful actions, with ability. Those capable of doing wrongfully will possibly do wrong. Those capable of thinking wrongfully will possibly think wrong.

On the matter of second chances, they are not inevitable. Their considerations, however, are.

Beg to differ on the opinions of those awaiting downfall. For those who crave such change shall inevitably, as all else, follow through.

…people, that is.

Warning: Recall

At journeys end we are reminded of the times well spent. In comparison to the trials at first sight, the now appears as the end. As time passed the reliables changed as often as the time, with the only exceptions being that of truths. For truths may change in shape and in error and in character but never in form. That which is true in one shape is true in another. That which is true in one error is true in another. As that which is true in one character is true in another.

On Love

Third degree cuts leave eternal wounds as reminders of
damage done.
Cry not of the causation more than once, for the scar
goes on.

New Born

The annual cleaning process approaches quickly and soon enough the anthems of the new years and subjective new "me's" shall ring along with the passing days of the new decade. For science's sake cut the crap.

The reinvention of the self requires realignment with new ideologies, a reification of all that was pleasant and noble while relinquishing all that was unpleasant and ignoble. Such a manifestations exists only if the minds of those willing to truly deny the self bodily pleasures in effort to feed the soul.

As it may be evident, babies feel pain as the blind can look into the souls of others in order to judge one's fulfillment. As the many have the understanding of an unfulfilled soul, only the few have knowledge of one fulfilled.

New Endeavors

With old dogs come histories filled with neither doubt nor misconception. The past is due to a lack of misunderstanding. All men hold faith in that is known.

With the new, comes: a lack of consistency, less understanding due to more doubt, more misconception. Only the noble have faith, for truth has not been seen.

Crystal balls and fairy tales end in manners many know all too well.

Though adequately terrified, I have faith. May truth be in my future and happiness a part of the plan.

στην έλλειψη (lack)

For the quality of life derives from a balance of truths and fantasies. For what one needs differs heavily from his wants.

Derivatives of truth and fantasy resemble a balance of the two.

One needs truth.
One wants fantasy.

In times of great uncertainty, lines of truth and fantasy are not as far. Occasionally, we all really need something we really want.

dickey c

Stand back…we are robots

Existing has its on little way of reminding one of our lacks of autonomy in life. We are notified of eviction just when the road appears to be clear and steady. In all my days of life, a feeling of control is a constant. Of course this requires not considering those moments where said power is lacking, which seem to come more often than the controlled.

In regards to understanding, the past seems simpler than the now and tomorrow. Reaching for hands that appear only inches away is the way.

Here and now is a time when many men have no agency. We are not acting, just happening. As these moments past more approach with agendas similar to those just gone.

Helpless. Yeah that's it. Helpless.

Transmission End.

愛のない (Ai no nai) - Loveless

To love another is to care less about the self. This is not a negative. The man who truly loves another cares about another more than himself. This is simple for one who understands how to love.

Acrophobia?

The trials of free falling into nothingness are a fear that I, unfortunately, know not enough about. My issues stretch farther to free falling into something of too much something-ness or controlled landing into places I know nothing about. At this point and time all I can truly relate to is the feeling of the letters W-T-F as my fingers ever so politely stroke them softly.

After years of consideration I have come to the conclusion that I suffer from a bad case of scared-height-syndrome. The falling is always different for me whether it be free falling or controlled. The trend has never been a constant when it regards to the downs. The element of being so high all the time is a fear that I, unfortunately, know all too much about. The ups are always up.

The idea of having too much fun or laughing too much or smiling all the time is so close to happiness that it causes fright in the upper left side of my chest. Imagine it…happiness. It's the one thing that we all strive for in life, the single thing that brings us all.

The idea of it all sickens me. Instead of embracing the highs of the ups I relinquish them by either jumping or easing my way back down. True as it may be, I may be in dire need of a roller coaster alcohol-anonymous equivalent.

I am afraid of heights.

On Friendship...

The saliva following the climax of sex and reality often craves a second serving. The satisfaction of finishing a collective of life long moments begs one to question, "why end?" A good picture leaves a great audience wanting the greatest love and unsatisfied are the people.

In a calling to abstract language, we spit in the faces of justice and cry tears of joy so that freedom answers a yearning for pleasure. Give them not what is required but what is begged for.

Cancer kills the body as the worse reputations assist the suicides of legacies of the best men. Unfortunately, to judge a man on heightened isolations renders very little logic. For the honored acted as the honored before them, habitually at least.

Once the truth…three times the black sun

We look at truth to be self evident to those factitious oppositions. For such oppositions exist vividly, whereas the truth, contrary to the common belief, exist as fairy-tales told to women and children alike.

To those men who speak the truth, we thank them for their nobility and just. For without those with such virtue we would have no factitious comparison.

To those men who speak lies, we banish them to a life worth living only till end. For because of those with such vice, we have only the noble to look on forward.

I once told another that I loved her. For this I was thanked once for my nobleness and beauty. Deemed once a man of good word, for once a beautiful man shall be beautiful only once.

I once told another I loved him. For this I was thanked a thousand times. Deemed always a liar, for once a man lacking nobleness and goodness shall always be as such.

On forgiveness…

The will to live alone is a desire held only by the strong at heart.
Both love and hate exists on opposing spectrum, for the fear around them both equates evenly.
Be not weary of those in love, but those waiting to forgive.

Help...

The constraints at which we operate consist of boundaries set aside by memories we allow to shape the world and the manner we view it.

For miles your worth illuminates with an ego as wide as the sun.

Namaste. I just tried to help and for that I am sorry.

Battle of sex...

Within all men exist passions. Concerns of their
existence are note-worthy but it is the concerns of their
co-existences that hold the most significance.

dickey c

The grab scheme…

On nights like tonight I come to conclusions of empathic perfections. I am well aware of my addictions.

The space held by love is one of inevitability. Caused by one whole affecting a minimal two souls.

tears

Across the Water

Sometimes too far is too far. In regards to limits the most interesting question questions the rate at which we reach the limit. When does too far become too far?

.

Beautiful contradictions

The beauties in life are the simplest complexities when concerning phenomena. Picking up trash in dresses, simply for love. Thinking again about decisions we've already made. Harming ourselves for the sake of another's well being. The wait is typically worth it. The phenomenon behind it all is so private and exhilarating that such experience cannot be explained, for the noblest and truest of acts can only be experienced.

On love

When love is considered, the truth is only a matter of fact.

dickey c

Intermission
Take a break

dickey c

Se muerte

with the likes of the latest wave circa 1990, the planning
for such a massive funeral was beyond due time. this
morning she removed his clothes and fucked him.

the screams of erotic combinations of pain and pleasure
evoked herds of questions with few calves to answer.
without regret, he took like a man.

before permission, but with consent, the safe bond that
was once shared among he and her was
excommunicated to make way for a newer, less manly
one. less doors opened, less chair pulled afar.

for she arrived here with open arms and farewell cards.
welcoming a new-2year contract while saying goodbye to
that old device.

may peace be with

dickey c

On necessity

in the circumstance of essentials, what one needs are
those that are life worthy.

One more time

so the latest episode in this anthology i call life has brought me to the realization that i don't have much more time to waste. we have spent so much time in different places without understanding how it affects us both. i want you, and you don't want to want me. you want me and i don't want to want you. call me crazy, but i believe that life is full of ups and downs, with the ups much higher than the downs. i have been on this down for so long that the feeling of every little up cause me to appreciate life just a little bit more. if i could take it all back, go back and do it all over again, i probably wouldn't. this has taught me so much over the the last four years, you have taught me so much. i have loved every moment. i keep telling myself that i was always nice, but the truth is, i wasn't i have done my share of wrong. i have done my share of damage. and for that i am sorry. this song keeps playing in my head…today it begins, i've missed it before, but won't miss it again. i keep having the same dream. and i think that i just realized what it means.

dickey c

Do something with your life

in the essence of simplicity one is often questioned, "how do I fit in?" My place is one so complicated that the truth may truly be further away than this fantastical imagery that has surfaced by my own fault. If love were simple would the fight be worth it? If love were worth it would the fights be worth it?

The fantasy, of course, includes a slight glare at what some would interpret as perfection. Similar to the truth, with fantasy, the mind acts without limits. The conflict exists within the difference between the two, for fantasy and truth are not interchangeable.

To act on fantasy as if it were truth is less noble then to act on truth as if it were fantasy. But it is acting on either truth or fantasy without the understanding truth that is the least noble. For unlike fantasy, the truth is bound with that that truly exist, tangibly that is.

For action, the man who acts is honored more than he who does nothing.
For truth, the man who understands is honored more than he who does not.
For life, the man who does nothing due to understanding of the truth is the noblest man, for the truth is bound by that that truly exists.

Shoot for the stars

common as it may be, many white men have changed
my life.

Instructed to reach for the stars sometime in my high
school career. As stupid as that may have sounded then,
and still does now, it pressured me to pressure myself.
The ideology of self-reflection is one that that has very
little value in comparison to its valor. one step back in
order to take the next step forward appears at eye level
ludicrous and proves to be so as to; ludicrous.

dreams are compared to egos…he who is willing to
acknowledge their existence has attained a lack of fear
of their nonexistence.

*shouts to Uncle Tom, may he be exalted.

On tolerance

As before, the truth is simply a matter of fact. When considering relationships, those including friends and the more and less, the truth should not affect perceptions. this is the difference between acceptance and tolerance.

Silly Rabbit

It's funny. That poor little rabbit represents a group of individuals that many alike can relate. He wanted something so bad, something simple, but was denied access to it. The passion he held regarding attaining what he wanted was completely relentless or resilient. But was it stupid?

The Rabbit has been chasing the same thing for so many years, not falling subject to pressure or defeat. Even though he has been denied what appears to be a love of his so many times, he continues strongly to fight for what he wants. But when is quitting time?

Aristotle counts the courageous man as one who understands his limits and fears in the right amount. Courage is the mean in between fearing too much and no fear at all. This Rabbit seems to fear nothing between him and his want for tricks, but I would say he's pretty courageous. The ability to keep fighting when facing defeat.

Now tricks may not appear to be the best example of tangible items worth fighting for, but what is?

We all fight for the most random of things. Typically we decide that they are important to us, important enough not to give up on. Losers give up, and we all want to win right?
But how much is too much? We all put up with crap on

top of crap just to be reminded that what we want is not happening. I am all for fighting. I have been in the same one for almost years now. But when is quitting time?

After a long deserved win or drawn-out defeat?

fingers

I like to stare. although some find it rude, it fulfills some awkward piece of my soul.

I like to point. although some find it rude, it fulfills some awkward piece of my soul.

I don't like to be pointed at. That is probably the rudest shit on earth.

There exist this complex that urges one to do unto others in hope that particular actions will be accepted, with the premise that said action will never be returned? Both pots and kettle are black…right?

dickey c

Washcloths and philosophy

For those just tuning in, I like to think. I am currently pursuing degree in the thought of thinking, or more commonly known as Philosophy. Firefox appears to care very little for my discipline. In an effort to correct the spelling of said discipline it suggested to replace my studies with the word **washcloth**. The truth is my understanding of what I am actually studying is so far away from complete that **washcloth** almost works.

It's not fair. Dora has a backpack with a map that gives her insight to where she and her trusty booted companion are headed. All I have is Mozilla hinting that maybe the work of my life is worthless. Well maybe not worthless but not nearly as worthwhile as let's say…one of those fancy beach towels.

What's worse, a lack of understanding of a self proclaimed path in life, or the lack of value given to said path by others?

Ventriloquist throw their voices. A talent reserved for the oppressed. Throwing voice requires understanding of the here and there. How one sounds here and how one will sound there. The moving from there to here promotes the individual but harms collective. Help here, or go there?

dickey c

I saw a documentary…

…on Antarctica. If all the ice melts…where will the
penguins dance?

ライオン (lion)

The refreshing tone of a friend makes me wonder... in a pool full of lies, just how much are false truths worth?

i learned to swim. through acts of light and refreshing courses of love, i learned.
in clear water and warmed air. i swam for hours.

awoke with the smell of sewage and drunken nights i was warned of failure. i forgot how to swim, in sludge and cold air. i swam for minutes.

in all the time we spent you lied, and now there exists a memory of false realities.

i think someone just broke into a car across the street.

Word to the wise?

the ancients spoke of one true immortal. not in
understanding, but in hopes to understand.

the poets stood by, and wrote not in hopes to
understand, but in understanding. pieces de love, honor,
power, man and the laws.

the ancients criticized such hopefuls, for they understood
not what they wrote, but wrote what they did not
understand. as for the philosophers, they in similar
fashions, spoke not what the knew, but what they craved
to know.

speaking of truths that i don't understand and being
respected, that of the poetry.
speaking of truths i know i don't understand and being
ridiculed, that of philosophy.

wisdom, or word to the wise?

Wake up

as thoughts of love from the future lead way through
mental canals created without purposes, questions of life
after love follow closely. lives after happiness beg
themselves for answering.

the existing state of death has not quite manifested into
existence. whether it be a debate of philosophy or
linguistics the dilemma is quite consistent…can death
be?

unfortunately, i am not sure.

i'll let you know when i'm dead

dickey c

On love...

with matters of the heart, gender has not much if no significance at all.

Tranquilo

miracles happen over night only in movies based on
fairytales.
you may say that im a dreamer…but I'm not.

dickey c

V1

do not what the heart asks of the soul.

i've come to a point of denial. as a unit, we have traveled
down the runway to the point of critical choice.

to fly in anguish hoping a safe return in other places, a
happier adventure.
to brake, stop, discontinue the idea of upward mobility
and hope that the runway is able to endure such a
sudden halt.

i wanna fly, but maybe i can't hold on to you.
slash…who wants to fall?

word

Aesthetics of contemporary music

lyrics in solitude is mere poetry.
for without the company of instrumentals we are
composed to enjoy misery.
i'd give my all for love...harmony.

Habla Loca

the truth is simply is matter of fact.

in the most fortunate cases these matters are simply
understood. adversity lingers over the many, for only few
are as fortunate as kings.

to live as the common and know as the kings is a quality
only held by an elite few, misguided by the fates of life.
fate employs these kings to guide the most common in
efforts to higher understanding.

with matters of fact, only those who are guided by those
with true understanding hold any chance of attainment of
happiness.

Flashlights and truths

sometimes when i'm alone i pretend i am skinny.

the rate of conception at which newer/better me's are created doubles daily, at least that's what it feels like in my head. the concept of the "Self" does not exist outside of perception; one can only imagine the self within a conception of the self.

yesterday i wore a blue shirt, or a red shirt, or a green shirt, or, if i was skinnier, possibly no shirt. my face was flawless, free of imperfections. my posture just perfect. my jeans: new with that "i wore these yesterday maybe" facade. the body constantly in action. the self constantly in action, within a perception. whether it be a matter of fact or fiction, the self exists both mentally and physically within a perception.

of course, i'd never pretend to be fat, for that would be nonsense.

Trees go bad

the feeling of familiarity sparks during times like this. as the rain pours down onto arms awaiting misery, the thought of curiosity is begged…"am I putting myself in the same situation again?"

with new love comes the unbalancing of a life. my life. I feel the discomfort of naivety. in all my reflection I learn only the simple things; mostly remembering dates and times. if I ever wrote a love song it would consist of lessons not learned and feelings not spoken for. if only I were smarter.

if perfection were a trait carried by few, this logic would rationale my love.
but perfection is a trait carried by none, and it is for this reason i feel like I've been here before.

I want for acceptance.
I fear that it may be too late. I want to go home.

on searching for a flightless bird

Thanks for reading.

www.ingramcontent.com/pod-product-compliance
Lightning Source LLC
Chambersburg PA
CBHW072148090426
42739CB00013B/3318